W9-BCF-164

A New Testament

A New Testament

Sherwood Anderson

BONI AND LIVERIGHT
New York mcmxxvii

FIRST PRINTING, MAY, 1927
SECOND PRINTING, JUNE, 1927

PRINTED IN THE
UNITED STATES OF AMERICA

Table of Contents

PAGE

DEDICATED

TO

HORACE LIVERIGHT

They talked and their lips
said audible words but the
voices of their inner
selves went on uninterrupted.

While you can see me you shall not have me.

While you can reach out your hand and touch my fingers you shall not know I am alive.

In the time of my death and decay life shall come out of me and flow into you.

A Young Man

AT TIMES, just for a moment I am a Cæsar, a Napoleon, an Alexander. I tell you it is true.

If you men who are my friends and those of you who are acquaintances could surrender yourselves to me for just a little while.

I tell you what—I would take you within myself and carry you around within me as though I were a pregnant woman.

One Who Looked Up at the Sky

IT WOULD be strange if, by a thought, a man could make Illinois pregnant.

It would be strange if the man who just left my house and went tramping off in the darkness to take a train to a distant place came here from a far place, came over lands and seas, to impregnate me.

¶ There is a testament out of life to the man who has just left my presence. There is a testament to be made to a woman who once held me in her arms and who got no child. There is a testament to be made to this house, to the sunshine that falls on me, to these legs of mine clad in torn trousers, to the sea and to a city sleeping on a prairie.

Testament

Containing songs of one who would be a priest

Song Number One

MY LIFE has passed into a coma of waiting but I wait no more intelligently than you. Sometimes as I walk in the streets a look of intelligence comes into my eyes. If I had not watched closely the eyes of my brothers I would be often deceived by what I see in my own eyes.

¶ It is only by going about in secret I can stumble into the pathway of truth. When truth has passed through the streets of a town or has walked on wet leaves in a forest there is a faint smell. It is blown about by the wind. I smell the footsteps of truth but I do not walk in the footsteps.

¶ I have recently thrown out of my arms the maiden placed there by my father—a liar.
I sit in a stone chair in a cold place.
I am beset by many pains.
Pain comes running to me out of the bodies of men and women.
I am bred out of the lusts of the world.
I am become the abiding place of little lustful thoughts that weave in and out of the minds of my people.

¶ It is only to comfort my solitude I whisper to myself it is thus the new man emerges. It is a thought to play with, a ball to bounce off the wall. I have whispered to myself that the new man emerges out of the womb of an engine, that his birth cry arises out of a clangor of sounds.
My thoughts are tossed back and forth on a wall.
As you sit with me you shall be compelled to share my fate.
All you who live in the valley have had sticks thrust into your eyes.

You are shepherds of blind sheep.
You shall sit in the chair of stone.
You shall sit in the narrow place.
You shall be pregnant.
You shall sit in the stone chair at night and the throbbing of iron cities shall be in the intricate veins of your being.
There are walls of stone.
There are walls faced with iron.
Between them you shall sit.

* * *

¶ The little tricks of my mind shall explain nothing to you. If I should dig myself a grave and bury myself by the light of a summer moon you would pass like a flitting shadow along the further side of the wall.

¶ It is, however, my desire to die in the midst of a more intelligent pain. My desire is as yet no more than a tiny white worm that lives under a sidewalk in an Illinois town.

¶ You shall not know my desire until you slip into my place in the chair.
The noises of the world are tremendous.
The walls of the cities throb.
There is a new song stuck in the brazen throats of the cities.
There is an American song.
There is a song nobody knows.

¶ There is a child born of an engine in a bed of stone. American cities are pregnant. You understand what I mean. My insanity is crystal-clear to you as you sit in the chair of stone. To you my insanity is a white streak of moonlight that falls across the smoke-begrimed streets of your city.

¶ My insanity is a slow creeping vine clinging to a wall.
My insanity is a white worm with a fire in its forehead.

* * *

¶ I write only to beguile the hours of the waiting. It is that I am whispering about. I have put my lusts into an iron cage at the side of the chair. I am watching the people who file up out of the valley to go like wavering shadows along the face of the wall.

¶ I sit patiently watching the small white thing that comes out of my body to creep on the face of the wall.

Song Number Two

¶ You lie in the arms of your beloved but you are not in the arms of your beloved. It rains. The rain pours out of a broken water-spout into an alleyway.

There is a threshing of feet in wet streets. The feet hurry along. They carry the bodies of people bouncing along.
It is my constant desire to draw close to you. My lover held me close and close but I have escaped. We understand each other. You also have drawn close to a warm body and felt white arms clutched about your neck.
Your tramp soul will fly out with me into the night, into the wind and the rain and the cities. The minor things do not matter to us. I am testifying to you. Presently you shall testify to me.
Your voice that is a testament shall be like driven raindrops in a city street.
Your voice shall be like the rustle of leaves torn by a storm from a tree.
You shall uproot yourself.
You shall come out of the ground with soil clinging to you.

* * *

We shall walk in many rains.
We shall whisper in many high winds.
We shall be blown like grasshoppers over the sea in a storm.

¶ If you assert your brotherhood to me we shall be lost to each other. It is when you are torn from your moorings and drift like a rudderless ship I am able to come near to you.

* * *

¶ My fancy belongs to a high tossing place.
My lover's arms wither away.
My lover has gone in distress to walk in the rain.
I have been blown out of myself to walk in the wind and the rain.

* * *

¶ You have come to me out of the arms of your lovers.
You have come to me out of your warm close place.
You have lost yourself in the nothingness.
You are a leaf tossed in a wind.
You are a blade of grass torn out of the ground.

Song Number Three

¶ My throat has not yet been choked by the dust of cities.
My mind is a Kansas tumble-weed. It rolls and bounces and skips on wide prairies. The wind tosses it about. It scatters its seed.
My spirit has not yet been imprisoned by walls of stone and iron.

My spirit makes its testament to you.
When I have died, when my body is dry and has blown away, the dust shall fly into your eyes.
When you have come past me out of the mouth of the womb there shall be no looking back. You will not know how that I have seen you going up and down.
Your voice that testifies emerges out of a thickness of flesh. It grows faint with weariness. You stagger in a drunken stupor along streets past my eyes.
I have watched like a little red fox that lies at the mouth of a hole.
The coyote runs in the moonlight over the plains.
The body of the brown bear that lives on the rim of the bowl sings as he goes out to seek food.
I am very young and very old.
I am unborn.
I lie at the mouth of the womb.
What I have understood is none of your doing. The secret lies in the fact that your ugliness is my own. I have not sought you. In seeking myself I have come upon you.
I have seen you in many places, in a hall ringing with the voices of speakers, in a procession going through the streets, in a

deep hole into which you had climbed to lay the foundations of a prison.
Your lips were swollen.
I saw you with your throat cut lying in an alleyway in a city.
An old newspaper had been drawn over your face.
In the morning you were in a tree where you had climbed to see the face of a god.
You were running in streets at noon with your hat in your hand.
The gods of insanity played upon you with thin nervous fingers.
I saw you filling a barn with corn. I saw you building machines and houses. I saw sweat in your eyes. I heard your voice telling little lies. You were a writer of books. You were a man who shod horses. You were a drunken man who sat upright in a bed to laugh at the stars.
I saw you as I lay at the mouth of the womb in the midst of the valley.
I saw you when I sought myself.
I heard your voice making testament when my voice died away in a stillness.

Song Number Four

¶You are a child who sleeps and throws his hands up over his head.
You are a strong man who walks in a

street at night. In the silence you hear little sounds.
You are a country girl and live in Nebraska. At evening you drive cows along a lane to your father's barn.

* * *

¶ I grope my way toward you in the darkness.
I feel my way along the face of a wall.
I gather little stones and lay them along the face of the wall.

* * *

¶ You are an old woman without teeth. In the stairway of an old building you sit. You whine at me. Why do you not arise and sing? Why do you not make a testament to me?

* * *

¶ You have forgotten that I crawled into your arms as you lay in a bed. You have forgotten that we walked in an orchard.

* * *

¶ You are very lame. You have a twisted foot. It is your occupation to sell newspapers in the street before a railroad station. Your fingers have become like fruit that has been lying a long time in the sun. Your voice testifies in the city. You cry aloud in the city.

¶ How gentle you were that time when together we saw the little shadows playing on the face of the wall. Do you remember how the tears ran out of your eyes?

* * *

¶ You are a small man sitting in a dark room in the early morning. Look, you have killed a woman. Her body lies on the floor. Your face is white and your hands tremble. A testament is creeping from between your teeth. It makes your teeth chatter.
You are a young man in the schools.
You walk up the face of a hill.
You are an insane driver of sheep.
You are a woman in a brown coat, a fish merchant in a village, a man who throws coal in at the mouth of a furnace, a maiden who presses the body of her lover against the face of the wall.
You are a bush.
You are a wind.
You are the gun of a soldier.
You are the hide that has been drawn over the face of a drum.
You are a young birch tree swaying in a wind.
You are one who has been slain by a falling tree in a forest.

Your body has been destroyed by a flying mass of iron in the midst of a battle.
Your voice comes up out of a great confusion.
Listen, little lost one, I am testifying to you as I creep along the face of a wall.
I am making a testament as I gather stones and lay them along the face of a wall.

The Man with the Trumpet

I STATED it as definitely as I could.
I was in a room with them.
They had tongues like me, and hair and eyes.
I got up out of my chair and said it as definitely as I could.

¶ Their eyes wavered. Something slipped out of their grasp. Had I been white and strong and young enough I might have plunged through walls, gone outward into nights and days, gone onto prairies, into distances—gone outward to the doorstep of the house of God, gone into God's throne room with their hands in mine.

¶ What I am trying to say is this...
By God I made their minds flee out of them.
Their minds came out of them as clear and straight as anything could be.

¶ I said they might build temples to their lives.
I threw my words at faces floating in a street.
I threw my words like stones, like building stones.
I scattered words in alleyways like seeds.
I crept at night and threw my words in empty rooms of houses in a street.
I said that life was life, that men in streets and cities might build temples to their souls.

¶ I whispered words at night into a telephone.
I told my people life was sweet, that men might live.

¶ I said a million temples might be built, that doorsteps might be cleansed.
At their fleeing harried minds I hurled a stone.
I said they might build temples to themselves.

Previously printed in "The Triumph of the Egg".

Hunger

ON farms the dogs bark and old women groan as they crawl into beds. The scraping feet of old men make a shuffling sound on the floors.

¶ In the cities the street cars rattle and bang. The motors make great moving rivers in streets.

¶ It is winter now but in the spring there will be flowers in the fields and at the edge of roadsides. The spring rains will wash thoughts away. There will be long-stemmed flowers reaching up from shaded places under the trees.

¶ I am no more true than yourself, no more alive than yourself.

¶ You are a man and I would take hold of your hand. You are a woman, I would embrace you. You are a child, I would be unashamed to stand in your presence. The flower that is myself has a long stem.

Death

I DO NOT belong to the company of those who wear velvet gowns and look at the stars. God has not taken me into his house to sit with him. When his house has burned bright with lights I have stayed in the streets.

¶ My desire is not to ascend but to go down. My soul does not hunger to float. I do not wish to pass out of the animal kingdom and into the kingdom of birds, to fold my wings and pitch into the arms of a wind that blows in from the sea. The voice of the wind does not call to me.

¶ When I am strong and the noise of the cities roars in my ears it is my desire to be a little mole that works under the ground.
I would creep beneath the roots of the grass.
I would go under the foundations of buildings.
I would creep like a drop of rain along the far, hair-like roots of a tree.

¶ When springs come and strength surges into my body I would creep beneath the roots of grasses far out into the fields.

I would go under fields that are plowed. I would creep down under the black fields. I would go softly, touching and feeling my way.

¶ I would be little brother to a kernel of corn that is to feed the bodies of men.

The Healer

MY body does not belong to me.
My body belongs to tired women who have found no lovers.
It belongs to half men and half women.
My body belongs to those who lust and those who shrink from lusting.
My body belongs to the roots of trees.
It shall be consumed with fire on a far horizon.
The smoke that arises from my burning body shall make the western skies golden.
My body belongs to a Virginia mob that runs to kill negroes. It belongs to a woman whose husband was killed in a railroad wreck. It belongs to an old man dying by a fire in a wood, to a negress who is on her knees scrubbing floors, to a millionaire who drives an automobile.

My body belongs to one whose son has killed a man and has been sent to a prison. It belongs to those who have the lust for killing and to those who kill.
My body is a stick a strong man has stuck in the ground. It is a post a drunkard has leaned against.
My body is a cunning wind. It is a thought in the night, a wound that bleeds, the breath of a god, the quavering end of a song.

Man Speaking to a Woman

YOU HAVE come to me from a tall awkward city. You have come to me from the sister cities of the north. On your way here to me you have run in and out of a thousand cities that lie like unhatched eggs on the prairies.

¶ You are a distraught woman with tangled hair and once you owned a house in a street where wagons and motor trucks went up and down.
I am glad you are tangled in a web of thought.
I am glad your thoughts have driven you out of the cities.

You have come up a hill to a place where I sit.
I am glad.
I will take the end of a thought in my hand and walk back and forth.
I will climb into trees.
I will run in holes under the ground.
I will weave a web over yourself.

You shall sit on a stone under a wall where a gateway leads into the valley of truth and as I weave you into oblivion I will tell you a tale.

Long ago, on a day in October, a woman like you came here to the face of the wall. The shadow of many perplexities lay like a film over her eyes. She sat on the stone with her back to the wall as you sit now. My father, who was then a young man, laid long threads of thought over her body.
A stone fell out of the wall and the woman was killed.
The wall is strong but a stone fell out of the wall.
It made a great noise.
A noise like the firing of guns was heard to the North and the South.

In the Valley there was a day set aside for the cleansing of doorsteps.

The sound of the tinkling of bells came over the wall.

A stone fell out of the wall on the head of a woman.

She fled from my father.

She fled like a frightened bird over the wall.

A Dreamer

I HAVE no desire to fathom the infinite. It is my desire to walk up and down in fields and forests and to knock with bare knuckles on the doorposts of houses. As I sit on a log at the edge of an Illinois town the factories and the houses in which things are bought and sold crumble into a dust so fine that my breath can blow it away.

¶ I live in a day and in a place where pigs are sold on the King's doorstep. What I know you also know. Foul smells arise out of the streets of my cities. The woman who passes me clad in a fur coat has a pair of handcuffs concealed under her gown.

¶ In my arrogant pride I have said to myself—I shall run through life like a little lost dog, I shall put my cold nose against the bodies of people.

¶ I have no end in life beyond that of a bare-legged boy who climbs into a leafy tree. I have a hope that when I have climbed to the topmost branch and have put out my hand it will for a moment graze the wings of a thought.

¶ I am a beggar and will accept any word you may choose to bring me. I am a man gone blind. I am an aged man with a beard who carries a staff and strikes with it on a pavement.
Someone has struck me a hard blow.
The drums of my ears have been destroyed by the scream of a whistle.

¶ It would be better for me to be a beggar on the doorstep of your house.

¶ I should be one who accepts the singing of the wind in the hair of one who has been hanged as the voice of a god. When you arise from your bed in the morning and come to your kitchen door you should find me sitting there with bowed head. I should be able to whisper to you a word out of the departed night.

¶ When I have grown beyond my love of God I shall grow in my comprehension of you.

¶ There shall be a way found by which I may go through a street to the door of God's house. I shall find words to lay on my lips. I shall find words to speak at the door of God's house.

Man Walking Alone

THE NIGHTS in the valley of the Mississippi River have the eyes of an owl. I have risen from the place where I slept under a tree but cannot shake the sleep out of my eyes. The nights in the valley of the Mississippi River are staring nights. They look at men with the pupils extended. The skies are empty over the cities and the plains. The skies have not formulated a thought that I can breathe into my being. In the whole valley of the Mississippi River there is no bed of thought in which I can lie.

¶ There are farm women living in houses that stand beside dusty roads in Illinois and Iowa. In Indiana and Ohio there are many towns. In Michigan—far up where the valley is no more and where the cold finger of the north touches the earth in September—there are men living who wear heavy boots and fur caps and who walk all day under naked trees.

¶ Everywhere are men and women who arouse wonder in me. I have awakened the feeling of wonder in myself. I have awakened from sleeping under a tree.

Testament of an Old Man

I AM AN old man sitting in the sun before the door of my house. The wind blows sharply, shaking golden leaves off the trees. It is late October and cold but I am not cold. My house protects me. The fingers of the wind cannot find me. The sun plays gently over my body. The dying fires within me are a little stirred. The blood mounts up through my body into my brain. My brain is fed with warm blood. It awakens.

¶ King David, when he was old, could not be warmed by the virgins lying with him in a bed but I am warmed by the soft kiss of the sun. The sun is my sweetheart. There is nothing in the world so fair as the sun. The sun is my virgin. The virgins that were brought to King David in old times looked at him and the blood did not mount into their bodies. They lay in bed with the King but they did not warm him. There was no warmth in them. My virgin, the sun, comes very close. She takes me into her arms. She warms me. The body of the sun is pressed close to my body. The sun's breath, fragrant with love, warms me.

¶ My brain that has been for many days asleep, runs madly. It runs down across plains. My brain is a hound that has come out of its kennel. It runs with long strides, swiftly, like a shadow. It runs as a shadow runs, swiftly, o'er wheat and corn fields, o'er towns and cities, o'er seas.

¶ My awakened brain is a hound dog come out of its kennel. It is a hound dog, white and silent and swift.

¶ My brain runs backward and forward, it runs on into cities the foundations of which have never been laid, it runs o'er fields that shall be planted at the hands of men not yet come from the womb, not conceived yet.

¶ My hound brain is a whispering wind. It runs backward and forward. It runs into new lives. It runs back into old lives.

¶ It has run beside Jesus the Prince as he walked alone on a mountain. It has lain all night at the door of a tent where Cæsar was encamped on a hillside in Gaul.

¶ My hound mind lay whining all night at the feet of the Cæsar. We ran out of the camp. We ran into cities. We ran to where Cæsar's wife lay in a bed. As Cæsar slept we groveled and fought with other dogs in the street of the mighty city of Rome.

¶ My hound mind has seen cities rise out of the plains and it has seen cities destroyed. It has seen tall oaks grow, mature and decay where Ruth went to glean in the harvest. It once lived in a slave who carried great stones to build a cathedral to the glory of God.

¶ My hound first came into my body when I was a lad tramping the fields. It went with me to live in the towns. Through a long life it has stayed in its kennel but now it is fleeing away.

¶ Look how it runs. O'er towns and cities it runs. It runs like a shadow o'er the seas. Some day it will not return to its kennel. My old body, now warmed by the sun, shall be put under ground. Old words will be said. Quivering voices shall sing quivering songs. My hound shall sit on its haunches and look. It shall forget and later remember.

The sun has warmed me. I call my hound back to me over the plains. I caress it. My voice is raised in a song. My house shakes with my cries. I spread banners afar, over the sky.

My hound mind has brought me the love of the gold. It has brought me the love of the lust. It has made me a proud man who walks on the bodies of slaves. It has taught me the lust of the purple robe, the lust of the lovely bodies of women.

Who knew as I walked among men how I lusted, what gold coins dripped from my fingers, how my blood was hot with the lust of war, of killing, of glory.

Who knew that I was a king walking the streets of a factory town, begging for bread, sleeping in straw.

With my hound asleep in its kennel I walked with a Cæsar. I played at battles with a Corsican corporal.

⁋ I lived in a factory town. I lived in the palace and walked in the park of a king.

⁋ Who knew that I made beautiful American cities. Who knew I planted purple and gold flowers on the ash heaps of cities.

⁋ Who knew how my soul knelt to the beauty of lives. Who knew how I knelt before lives, how like a white Christ I hungered and loved my way into lives.

⁋ My hound mind has been into the mountains with Jesus. It has been with the gentle Confucius. It has been with all gentle men.

⁋ It has been with the mighty and proud. It has been with those who slew in the darkness and threw the knife into a bush. It has been with those who stole money at night, with a boy who crept into a barn lusting alone, with a woman who opened softly the door to look for her lover.

⁋ I am a man who sits in the sun before the door of his house. My body grows old. The hinges creak on the door of the kennel. My hound mind runs out over the plains. It runs backward and forward. It has run back into lives. It runs on into new lives.

¶ King David could not be warmed by the virgins that crept with him into a bed but my sweetheart the sun has brought warmth into my body.

¶ I shall call my hound back to me over the plains. I shall caress it. My voice shall be raised in a song. My house shall shake with my cries. I shall spread banners afar over the skies.

Half-Gods

THE LITTLE half-gods are whining in the street. The strong medicine of life has burned their bellies and their skins are wrinkled. Their bones have become brittle and their voices weak. They are too cold and too young. Words without meaning drop from their lips.

¶ In the attempt to walk on the rim of life the half-gods have made themselves engines of steel. The air is befouled. The children of men choke in the streets.

¶ My ears are befouled. I have got a disease from sitting with half-gods in a room. My clothes are befouled by the stench of the engines.

Ambition

I AM ONE who has walked out of a tall building into the streets of a city and over plains into a forest that fringes a river. My notion is one of escape. I can no longer bear the life led in my father's house. I am a child and cannot escape out of my childhood. There is a door through which I cannot enter, a wall I cannot climb. The idea of escape long ago attacked the seat of my reason—a quaint fancy as well enough I know that such a thing as reason cannot exist.

¶ In the streets of a city, after I had walked out at the window of a tall building, a man came to walk with me. He held a small stick in his hand and twirled it over his finger. He said God would forgive me my transgressions if I would go in at the door of God's house and cease walking up and down.

¶ God lies on the ground in the forest with his head at the base of a tree.
The fingers of God flutter like the wings of a gnat.
A little leaf in the forest, touched by the

finger of God, whirls and twists in an agony of delight.
I have bathed in a stream and walked up and down on prairies.
I have been lying at full length in Illinois.
I have put my hands into Iowa, into Kentucky, into Indiana, Kansas, Ohio, Nebraska, the Dakotas.

¶ My mind is the mind of a little man with thin legs who sells cigars in a store.
My mind is the mind of a cripple who died in an alleyway at Cleveland, Ohio.
My mind is the mind of a child who fell into a well, the mind of one who cleans the streets of a city, of an actor who walks up and down on a stage.

¶ I double my fists and strike the ground a sharp blow. Ridges of land squirt out through my fingers.
I have remade the land of my fathers.
I have come out of my house to remake the land.
I have made a flat place with the palms of my hands.

In a Workingman's Rooming House

AT TWO o'clock at night a steamboat whistle blows in the Chicago River. A man who lives above me gets out of bed and goes barefooted across the floor. His feet fall on the boards like the fingers of a player on a silent piano filled with broken strings.

¶ He strikes a match. I know what he is doing. He is lighting a candle in order that God may see into his room and remember him in the time of his death.

¶ I do not arise and light a candle for the sake of God. I lie still and think. God has multiplied himself so often in my sight that I cannot see him by the light of a candle.

A Man Standing by a Bridge

FOR A long time I had the illusion I was helping to build a house. A wind has blown the illusion away. Building is going on but I have nothing to do with it. It may be that you are the builder.

¶ I am perplexed with trying to find out who does the building. I creep in the dusty hallways and hear many strange voices. The voices of men and women resound out of the darkness.

¶ The voices cry out to me that they are the voices of builders but as I go forward, feeling with my hands on the walls, I do not come to the place of the building.

¶ A soft voice has whispered to me that there is no such thing as a builder. It was a woman's voice. "The noise you hear is made by heavy untruths in the hands of arrogant men. The men lean out of a window. They beat on a brazen sky. They are trying to make holes in the sky."

The Red-Throated Black

GIVE me the word.
Let my red throat and black lips caress the words of your lips.

Give me the word.
Give me three words, a dozen, a hundred, a history.
Give me the word.

Give me the word.
Throw a curse at my head.
Throw a threat at my eyes.
Give me the word.

Give me the word.
I will melt song into your words.
I will color your words with song.
I will eat your words and vomit forth song.
Give me the word.

Put a sweet word under my tongue.
My blood is still hot.
The word shall take root. It shall grow.
It shall flower.
Give me the word.

I shall breathe perfume into your words.
I shall make a new word of your word.
My throat is a hot womb in which the seeds of words have been sown.

¶ Give me the word.
Give me your God.
Give me the Lord God.
Give me Saul and David.
Give me Bildad and Shuhite.
Give me the word.

¶ Give me the stinging end of a whip.
Give me your Christ that died.

¶ Give me the word.
Give me the word.
Give me the word.

¶ Let me put my hands on the word.
Let me touch my red tongue to the word.

¶ Give me the Lord.
Give me the Lord God.

¶ Give me sweet words. Give me profane words.
My throat hungers for words.
My throat is the womb of song.
My lips shall lap the red wounds of song.

¶ Give me the word.
Give me the word.
I am the singer.
Give me the word.

Singing Swamp Negro

I'LL BRING tears to your eyes with song,
Let me sing.
When I am gone, when I have consumed the poison my song shall roll and echo along rivers,
It shall roll through the graveyards of forests,
O'er fields,
Along deserted wharfs, where ships rot in the sun,
In swamps,
In deserted cabins,
In the hearts of the brethren—gone white.
Let me sing.
Did you hear me singing at night—in the morning? Did you know I was the soul of song?
Did you hear the song singing in my legs, my feet, my back, my arms?
Did you hear the wild song, the true song?
Did you see song come into life? Did you see it play up and down the black skin of my back?
Let me sing.

I was the song.
I sang as a fish swims. I sang light into dark places.
I took hold of the hand of the mother of song.
I took hold of the hand of the mother of sorrow.
I danced in the night under a moon.
Let me sing.
I am the Christ you crucified.
Why did you bring me the Christ that died?
Let me sing.
I am the song that does not die in the throat. I am myself the sweet inner meaning of song.
Let me sing.
I will bring tears to your eyes with song.
My hands are building the tomb of song.
Song is dying in me.
Let me sing.

Thoughts of a Man Passed in a Lonely Street at Night

I HAVE gone to walk up and down. It is night and cold. I want to creep into you. You have made me by thinking of me and I declare you should be ashamed of what you have done.

¶ Why have you not made me more pure? Why have you not made me more beautiful?

¶ Your conception of me makes me a little ill. It forces me to run away from you into a field of fancy, into a forest of doubt. If I cannot be one who when weary lies in warm human layers of thought I shall become for the nonce and until I am rested something not human. I have passed out of your presence.

¶ I will multiply myself until I pass like a vapor out of your mind.

¶ I am a thing hung suspended in life.

¶ There is no life in me, only a desire to creep into your arms and sleep after my long walking up and down.

Cities

THE NOTION of becoming a Jeremiah pleases my childish fancy. I shall be a Jeremiah in the mood that comes over God when he amuses himself by tickling a solitary leaf in a forest.

¶ I shall walk a long way and sit down in the grass. When night comes I shall weep. The hot tears that run out of my eyes shall make a little stream in which fishes shall live.

¶ My tears shall be many and shall make a broad river over which birds shall fly in the light of a morning.
My tears shall mature a stalk of corn that shall feed a little mouse that shall nibble forever at the foundations of buildings within which the fancies of men have decayed.

A Youth Speaking Slowly

I STAND here on a prairie near a town. Do you understand that distance has always been there, before me, that I breathe distance, that it flows through me like a prairie wind?
There is Europe there, and Africa and the land of the Russ. I hear voices out of your places but they remain voices. I shall never touch the flesh or soul of you. I put you aside. You are not in my distance, that I know.
I step three paces forward then I stop.
The wall recedes and stops before me.
In what way does it matter?
You are there at the edge of another town.
You are in a cornfield.
You are in the streets of Denver looking over the vast rim of my bowl.
You are in the Alleghany Mountains looking down at me.
You are in any city of the plains looking out at a factory window or out at the window of a house.
Houses and factories are but symbols to us. They are toys that amuse our children because they are so small in our vast place.

It is my passionate desire to shatter distances.

It is my passionate desire to distill, to condense.

Push my wall over and a world will be destroyed and new worlds will emerge.

It is only because I am so young that I push with my feeble arms against the face of the wall.

One Who Sought Knowledge

THERE are just as many things to be found out as anyone knows. No one I have ever met or talked with knows very much.

¶ Books are not such great things and most writers of books are fools. Believe me that is true. How many books I have read. How many singers I have gone to hear sing. How many times I have gone to galleries to see what paintings painters have painted.

¶ Life has not advanced very far. We do not need to be afraid we will be late to the battle.

The Minister of God

I WAS on my knees at prayer in a quiet dark place when lust for women came to me.

A Persistent Lover

IT IS EARLY morning and you and I have shaken the sleep out of our bodies and have renewed our covenant. We have struck with the flat part of our hands the face of the wall. We have bowed our heads in the midst of a cloud of vapor. By the strength of our understanding and by that alone we now stand on our feet.

¶ We stand upon our feet in the midst of the waters.

¶ The hillside and green stretches of country, that yesterday seemed to draw near, have receded out of our sight. In our place the grey surface of the waters runs in little ridges, changing color a little as the years pass and the days pass.

¶ The waters go on. In their never-ending movement the waters achieve the insanity we seek in vain. There is a persistent roaring noise, but the waters do not break upon the rocks. In the air above our heads sound breaks against sound. The hammering voices have not stopped since the forgotten dawn long ago when I found you standing alone.

¶ In the morning at the break of dawn there is a moment of quiet. The noises do not cease but there is quiet.

¶ In the evening when the day runs like a frightened rabbit into the hole of night there is quiet.

¶ It would be a comfort to me to know that at this moment at the beginning of our day our minds run together.

¶ It would be a comfort to me to know that as your mind runs like a tardy streak of light at the heels of night my mind also runs.

¶ It would be a joy to me to know that our two minds plunge forward together into the receding distance, over the waters.

¶ In my perplexity I lift my foot out of the firm sand at the bottom of the river and then set it slowly down.

My head rocks from side to side.

My hands are like branches of trees.

My hands are like the mottled backs of poplar trees that stand upright in a snow-storm that blows down a hill.

¶ I look at my hands and think of minute physical things concerning myself because I am loath to begin again thinking of you.

When I lift my eyes the day will be here.
I will see the wet strands of hair falling across your breasts.
Your tired eyes will look into mine.

¶ The uselessness of all effort will be indicated by the droop of your shoulders. An impulse toward love will tighten the cords of my throat.

¶ I will note again the nakedness of you, the smallness of the trunk of your body, the way the corners of your mouth twitch with weariness.

¶ The lids of your eyes are always very heavy and grey in the shifting light at the beginning of a day.

¶ How would it be with me if I could ride like a passenger on the back of your mind.

¶ When I have tried we both sank out of sight under the waters.

¶ Your mind should have been a boat in which we could lie together, sleeping and resting, but I am afraid then I should have become truly insane and run away in the night.

¶ It has not gone well with us as we walked, going ever more and more slowly forward into the drifting current of days. We have walked too long on the face of the waters. More than once I have kept silent when I wanted to thrust you away, out of my sight.

¶ Had I raised my hand to strike, our two hands would have met in the air above the waters.

¶ There would have been a more and more terrible hammering of sound against sound.

¶ Had I raised my hand to strike, my hand would have met your hand also intent upon striking.

¶ You have hidden yourself from me with lovely assurance.

¶ I did not want to know the thoughts that came to you in the midst of the day.

¶ I wanted your thoughts put away.

¶ Your legs have grown blue and as we stand in the waters my own legs have grown brittle.
The dawn has come.

¶ The hammering of sound against sound begins in the air over our heads.

¶ I raise my eyes to your eyes.
In a moment perhaps words will come to my lips.
In a moment, my beloved, I shall tell you anew the story of how, in a grey dawn long ago, I found you standing alone.

The Visit in the Morning

IT was by the sea—
I was lying on my belly and God came and turned me over.
He turned my face out of the sand, the yellow sightless sand.

℄ God caressed me and his caress was gentle and soft.
Out of my eyes he took what was sightless,
Out of my ears deafness.

℄ It has been permitted me to live and that was sweet before your time.

℄ The Divine inheritance God gave in the morning.
He kissed my lips, my breasts, my arms,
Then my lips again.

℄ Have you walked by a mountain?
Have you walked by the sea?

℄ I have been in the veins of the mountains.
I have been in each drop of water God spat out of his mouth.
A wind blowing out of my ears troubled the waters of the seas.

℄ God came to me as a bird comes out of a bush—softly—into a breaking day.

℄ God came to me in a glaring light.

℄ I have gone into you.
I have become of you.
In my pocket is the key to your house.
In my veins your blood flows.
The breath of you inflates my lungs.
The sweetness of you sleeps in my sleep.

¶ If you do not understand what I am saying that is of no importance.
That the winds blow in trees and that deaf men walk under the branches leading the sightless is of no importance.

¶ I was by the sea when God came to me.
He turned me over, turned my face out of the eyeless yellow sand.
He kissed my lips and I became alive.

The Dumb Man

THERE is a story. I cannot tell it. I have no words. The story is almost forgotten but sometimes I remember.

¶ The story concerns three men in a house in a street. If I could say the words I would sing the story. I would whisper it into the ears of women, of mothers. I would run through the world saying it over and over. My tongue would be torn loose. It would rattle against my lips.

¶ The three men are in a room in a house. One is young and dandified. He continually laughs.

¶ There is a second man who has a long white beard. He is consumed with doubt but occasionally his doubt leaves him and he sleeps.

¶ A third man there is who has wicked eyes and who moves nervously about the room rubbing his hands together.
The three men are waiting, waiting.

¶ Upstairs in the house there is a woman standing with her back to a wall, in half darkness by a window.

¶ That is the foundation of the story. Everything I will ever know is distilled in it.

¶ I remember a fourth man came to the house, a white silent man. Everything was as silent as the sea at night. His feet on the stone floor of the room where the three men were made no sound.

¶ The man with wicked eyes became like a boiling liquid. He ran back and forth like a caged animal. The old grey man was infected by his nervousness. He kept pulling at his beard.

¶ The fourth man, the white one, went upstairs to the woman.
There she was—waiting.

¶ How silent the house was. How loudly all the clocks in the neighborhood ticked.

¶ The woman upstairs craved love. That must have been the story. She hungered for love with her whole being. She wanted to create in love. When the white silent man came into her presence she sprang forward. Her lips were parted. There was a smile on her lips.

¶ The white one said nothing. In his eyes there was no rebuke, no question. His eyes were as impersonal as stars.

¶ Downstairs the wicked one whined and ran back and forth like a little lost hungry dog. The grey one tried to follow him about but presently grew tired and lay down on the floor to sleep. He never awoke again.

¶ The dandified fellow lay on the floor too. He laughed and played with his tiny black mustache.

¶ I have no words to tell what happened in my story. I cannot tell the story.

¶ The white silent one may have been death.
The waiting eager woman may have been life.

¶ Both the grey bearded man and the wicked one puzzle me. I think and think but do not understand them. Most of the time I do not think of them at all.

¶ I keep thinking about the dandified man who laughed all through my story. If I could understand him I could understand everything. I could run through the world telling a wonderful story. I would no longer be dumb.

¶ Why was I not given words? Why was I not given a mind? Why am I dumb? I have a wonderful story to tell but know no way to tell it.

Previously printed in "The Triumph of the Egg".

A Poet

IF I COULD be brave enough and live long enough I could crawl inside the life of every man, woman and child in America. After I had gone within them I could be born out of them. I could become something the like of which has never been seen before. We would see then what America is like.

A Man Resting from Labor

THIS TREE on which I am sitting in the forest fell down here and lies slowly rotting. Little crawling worms live in it. They are crawling near where I sit. The tree was not afraid or ashamed to fall down. The tree was not afraid or ashamed to grow or to die.

¶ The sunlight comes down through the leaves of these trees unafraid and unashamed.

¶ The wind blows when it does blow.

A Stoic Lover

I SAW HER little figure near the wall. She did not see me though she sensed my presence. I was like a statue with folded hands and she was like a little dog with quivering flanks that coldly waits beside a farmhouse door.

¶ Such a tiny thing she was.
She whined and with her fingers scratched the wall.
Her shaking flanks made a kind of music too.

¶ It was not winter.
Spring came on. The lovely breath of spring blew in her face. She whined and scratched the wall.

¶ I saw her nervous fingers making towns and streets. She played at living desperately. She built and built, caressed her own breasts, then fell to tearing at the wall.

¶ I sat stone still and watched.
Her quivering flanks set up a tremor in my frame.
My body shook and dust fell down from my eyes.
I moved and lived and felt the breath of spring and life blow in my face.

A Young Jew

YEARS and a life of it,
  Sitting in a room,
Walking with my father in a street,
Hungering,
Hating,
Burning my flame out in an empty place.
The smoke from burning bodies goes straight up.

Fire everywhere.
My world is choked with smoke of burning men,
With smoldering fumes of fires,
With smoke of burning men.
My mother's eyes look out at burning men,
At men who burn out in an empty place.
My mother's breasts are tipped with flames.
She has suckled men in fire.
She has suckled me in flames.
Her breasts are tipped with flames.
My mother's eyes look out at burning men.
My father's eyes look back at old things burned and charred.
They are hungering in the streets,
Their eyes are tipped with flames,
Their eyes flee from their bodies,
hungering in the streets.

The Story Teller

TALES are people who sit on the doorstep of the house of my mind.
It is cold outside and they sit waiting.
I look out at a window.
The tales have cold hands.
Their hands are freezing.
A short thickly-built tale arises and threshes his arms about.
His nose is red and he has two gold teeth.

¶ There is an old female tale sits hunched up in a cloak.

¶ Many tales come to sit for a moment on the doorstep and then go away.
It is too cold for them outside.
The street before the door of the house of my mind is filled with tales.
They murmur and cry out, they are dying of cold and hunger.

¶ I am a helpless man—my hands tremble.
I should be sitting on a bench like a tailor.
I should be weaving warm cloth out of the threads of thought.
The tales should be clothed.

They are freezing on the doorstep of the house of my mind.

¶ I am a helpless man—my hands tremble.
I feel in the darkness but cannot find the doorknob.
I look out at a window.
Many tales are dying in the street before the house of my mind.

Previously printed in "The Triumph of the Egg."

A Thinker

I SEE YOU, my beloved, sitting in a room beside me but I cannot speak to you. There is not time. You are young now but when I have turned my head to blow the smoke from before my eyes you shall grow old. I do turn my head again. You are a mumbling old woman. It is useless to speak to you. You are full of memories, crammed with them. There is no room for me to enter into you.

¶ It is quite true my beloved that I have always seen you as through a glass darkly. I see all life so.

¶ You are floating in a medium outside my own. That must be quite apparent. All men and women I have ever seen were floating in a medium outside my own. I a little understand the necessity for that—now. The day for the cure has not come. The time when God will breathe life into our nostrils lies lost in the future.

¶ That I have touched you and others with my hands, held you in my arms, caressed your tired eyes, awakened at night to see you asleep beside me—all facts, beliefs, suspicions, touching our belief in the reality of any approach we have made to each other are myths, fairy tales we have whispered to ourselves in the darkness of long nights. I believe that.

¶ However there is something more curious than what I am now saying to you. The fact of the impossibility of an approach to each other is so obviously curious. It is curious as the formation of a cliff may be curious. It is puzzling as the slippery, exhausted cross rhythms of waves are puzzling. You have seen the waves run on when the wind died on the face of the sea. You have seen many things I have seen.

¶ We have not approached the time when we may speak to each other but in the mornings, sometimes I have heard, echoing far off, the sound of a trumpet.

¶ It is apparent that nations cannot exist for us. They are the playthings of children, such toys as children break from boredom and weariness. The branch of a tree is my country. My freedom sleeps in a mulberry bush.

¶ What remains that is articulate is simply my desire to express to you something out of the now, the present. It is morning and you have gone, quite nude, to bathe on a beach. I see you there and you are lovely. Your head is turned a little to one side. Listen. I have put the bugle to my lips. Do you hear faintly the sound of it, running on the face of the waters. How stupidly I blow the trumpet. There is no music in me.

¶ I consume myself in my own attempt to find myself. It is thus I die, hourly, in every moment.

¶ You must understand however that it is my desire to communicate to you something out of the now, the present.

¶ I am a sea and a wind sweeps across the face of me. My words are little waves, thrust up. They are attempts to grasp, to lay hold of a passing thing. My words have, I well know, little to do with the actuality of you and of me.

¶ Yesterday a disease attacked the fields here, back of my house. A million winged grasshoppers descended upon the field. As I walked they arose in clouds. The grass in the field has become suddenly brown and dead. What was green has become brown, an ashy grey. Tomorrow another disease, a trick of the wind, a match thrown into dead grass will carry the grasshoppers away.

¶ It is true that you and I have looked about us a little. We have seen how empires are formed and civilizations crushed as a grasshopper is crushed under foot. There would be tragedy in that if empires or civilizations mattered to us.

¶ If I am a sea into which you may throw things there is a purpose in that. It is that things may be thrown into me that I exist.

¶ Let us return to yourself and myself. We stand here, now, in this instant, in the presence of the breathing sea that is myself, yourself, we are in the presence of a wind that runs, we are at the head of a street, watching the people pass, we are in a forest under trees.

¶ How strong, how swift, how sure we are. The grasshopper in flight, the gull twisting and turning in the air currents over a sea—nothing that lives is more strong and sure than ourselves. There is nothing in life superior to ourselves. We are ourselves superior to nothing in life.

¶ I have a passionate hunger to take a bite out of the now—the present. The now is a country to discover which, to be the pioneer in which I would give all thought, all memories, all hopes. My ship has but skirted the shores of that country. What is growing there? I would take a bite out of the present. I would consume it quite. I would live my life in the present, in the now only.

¶ For that purpose I would be ageless, impotent, potent, swift, a sluggish slow crawling worm, a singing rhythmical thing beating my wings, carried along for an instant in the flight of time. I would myself create a lull in the storm that is myself. I am a stream gone dry. Fill me with living waters. There is something stagnant in me. As I write, breathe, move back and forth in this room life is passing from me. Do you not see how I pass from one present into another unknowing. I would leave nothing unknown. To live in the presence of the unknown is death to me.

℄ Memories constantly create the disease of misunderstanding. It is the disease that shall destroy you and me. Only in the present, the now, is there awareness. All memories are disease. They corrupt, pervert life. They are clouds descended upon the clear sky. They shut out the sun. By their presence we are made blind.

℄ I would testify always out of the present and have come to realize that my ambition is a vain thing—an impossible dream.

℄ How often have I seen your face, a thousand faces passing in the street, in a street of the city of my mind. A face came toward me. It was unconscious of me. I was conscious of it and at the same time unconscious. The face spoke to me in the language of the instant, the now, the present. Golden words fell from lips that were ripe with life. The words were strong arms that lifted me up. What unspoken words I have heard.

¶ I tell you there is a language of which it may be said that every word in it comprehends more than all I have ever written, thought, dreamed. There is a country in which suns stand still. Hope is not dead. There is something living in you, in me.

¶ The words of those I have seen passing through the land of the now, the present, created as they went. They were pregnant words throwing off children as the sun throws off light.

¶ In my own person, and later I began to think, to remember. The glorious and living present became corrupt. It passed from me.

¶ It is not true that God created the world in six days, or rather perhaps he did—a fact that would account for the corruption of the world. Worlds should be created as gestures of gods.

¶ As I cannot live in the present, stay in it, it is impossible I should approach you. I am impotent. I cannot swim, fly, propel myself forward swiftly enough.

¶ Time has departed from me. What I was I shall never be again. What I may be today, tomorrow, cannot matter to you. You cannot grasp me now. I cannot lay hold of the fact of you.

¶ We were aware but we were but half aware. The bugle blew but we did not arise from our sleep. Even as I write the now, the present is passing from me. In a moment I shall begin to think, to remember. What is corrupt, corroding shall enter into me. Although I have died many times I shall in a moment and as you stand looking repeat over again the death scene I constantly strive to escape.

The Man in the Brown Coat

NAPOLEON went down into a battle riding on a horse.

Alexander went down into a battle riding on a horse.

General Grant got off a horse and walked into a wood.

General Hindenburg stood on a hill. The moon came up out of a clump of bushes.

¶ I am writing a history of the things men do. I have written three such histories and I am but a young man. Already I have written three hundred, four hundred thousand words.

¶ My wife is somewhere in this house where for hours I have been sitting and writing. She is a tall woman with black hair turning a little grey. Listen, she is going softly up a flight of stairs. All day she goes softly doing the housework in our house.

¶ I came here to this town from another town in the state of Iowa. My father was a house-painter. I worked my way through college and became a historian. We own this house in which I sit. This is my room in which I work. Already I have written three histories of peoples. I have told how states were formed and battles fought. You may see my books standing straight up on the shelves of the libraries. They stand up like sentries.

¶ I am tall like my wife and my shoulders are a little stooped. Although I write boldly I am a shy man. I like being in this room alone at work with the door locked. There are many books here. Nations march back and forth in the books. It is quiet here but in the books a great thundering goes on.

* * *

Napoleon rides down a hill and into a battle.
General Grant walks in a wood.
Alexander rides down a hill and into a battle.

* * *

℄ My wife has a serious, almost stern look. In the afternoon she leaves our house and goes for a walk. Sometimes she goes to stores, sometimes to visit a neighbor. There is a yellow house opposite our house. My wife goes out a side door and passes along our street between our house and the yellow house.

℄ The window before my desk makes a little framed place like a picture. The yellow house across the street makes a solid background of yellow.

℄ The side door of my house bangs. There is a moment of waiting. My wife's face floats across the yellow background of the picture.
General Pershing rode down a hill and into a battle.
Alexander rode down a hill and into a battle.

¶ Little things are growing big in my mind. The window before my desk makes a little framed place like a picture. Every day I wait staring. I wait with an odd sensation of something impending. My hand trembles. The face that floats through the picture does something I do not understand. The face floats, then it stops. It goes from the right hand side to the left hand side then it stops.

¶ The face comes into my mind and goes out. The face floats in my mind. The pen has fallen from my fingers. The house is silent. The eyes of the floating face are turned away from me.

¶ My wife is a girl who came here from Ohio. We have a servant but she sweeps the floors and sometimes makes the bed in which we sleep together. We sit together in the evening but I do not know her. I cannot shake myself out of myself. I wear a brown coat and I cannot come out of my coat. I cannot come out of myself. My wife is very silent and speaks softly but she cannot come out of herself.

¶ My wife has gone out of the house. She does not know that I know every little thought of her life. I know about her when she was a child and walked in the streets of an Ohio town. I have heard the voices of her mind. I have heard the little voices. I heard the voices crying when she was overtaken with passion and crawled into my arms. I heard the voices when her lips said other words to me as we sat together on the first evening after we were married and moved into this house.

¶ It would be strange if I could sit here as I am doing now while my own face floated across the picture made by the yellow house and the window.

¶ It would be strange and beautiful if I could meet my wife, come into her presence.

¶ The woman whose face floated across my picture just now knows nothing of me. I know nothing of her. She has gone off, along a street. The voices of her mind are talking. I am here in this room as alone as any man God ever made.

¶ It would be strange and beautiful if I could float my face across a picture. If my floating face could come into her presence, if it could come into the presence of any man or any woman that would be a strange and beautiful thing to have happen.

* * *

Napoleon went down into a battle riding on a horse.
General Grant went into a wood.
Alexander went down into a battle riding on a horse.

* * *

Some day I shall make a testament unto myself.

* * *

¶ I'll tell you sometimes the whole life of this world floats in a human face in my mind. The unconscious face of the world stops and stands still before me.

¶ Why do I not say a word out of myself to the others? Why in all our life together have I never been able to break through the wall to my wife? Already I have written three hundred, four hundred thousand words. Are there no words for love? Some day I shall make a testament unto myself.

Previously printed in "The Triumph of the Egg".

One Puzzled Concerning Himself

I HAD BEEN to the flesh pots all night—standing beside them, walking back and forth in the moonlight. I had gorged myself. My body was distended.

¶ I walked home to the city at dawn.
The moonlight was gone.
The streets were empty.
The voice of a drunken man shouted from an alleyway.

¶ I was smug brother to fat men.
I was tired but fattened.
I had been at the flesh pots.

¶ All night the moonlight fell down like rain on the roofs but I stayed at the pots, gorging myself.

¶ In the midst of the night as I walked, feeling myself full and complete, a child cried and its little voice, filled with strangeness in the quiet place, ran under the low black trees.

¶ The voice found no empty place in me. There was no vacant place where it could echo and reecho.

I was full and complete.
I had been gorging myself at the flesh pots.

The Dreamer

THE FANCY comes to me that thoughts like layers of smoke are lying along the street through which I have been walking. There are always banks of smoke hanging in the streets of my city. There is a sensual gratification to me in the notion that the crowds of men and women who have just passed me and who have gone before me have also lost themselves in the thoughts I have been lost in. By indirection I have been making love to all the men and women of a city.

¶ I am one who has no yesterdays and gropes dreamily toward a tomorrow. I am like you. You are not at all the thing you have so foolishly imagined yourself to be. I am nothing. I believe nothing. I would like to walk with you. If possible I would like to imagine you beautiful while you are in my presence. By indirection I wish to caress you, to touch with soft fingers the lids of your eyes, to lie like a gem in the hollow of your hand. For the moment that is the height of my desire.

℃ Many people have walked before me in the street, having as I have declared had a sort of intercourse with me. Before me, as I walked, in the forefront of my fancy, went a trembling old man. Ahead of him was a glorious woman, full breasted, strong at the shoulders. The wind blew her skirts and I saw that her legs were shapely and strong. She did not know that I knew what she was thinking about.

℃ Before the old man and the strong beautiful woman went many others in the canyon of the street. They walked like myself under the smoke pall of the city and like myself they walked in and out of the layers of thought. They were all like myself fanciful folk. They were making—each of them—designs in the darkness. In the dark street they felt for the threads of life with the fingers of their hands.

℃ How very many people going in and out of the thoughts. I fancied that I found a blank, a vacant place. Some brash impertinence out of my conscious life made me want to attempt to fill the blank.

¶ "I will put in this blank place a thought, a thought of my own," I said. It will be passed through by men, women and children. I crept into a doorway and watched, hoping childishly that the whole rhythm of the universe would be changed.

¶ Nothing happened of course, I suspect because my act was more than half conscious. My thought had no strength of its own. The wind blew it away.

¶ The streets of the city are roaring whirling places. Shrill human cries run like brightly colored threads through the thoughts of every man and woman who walks abroad. It is very foolish to try to be definite as I was as I attempted to lay down the thought. Nothing is to be achieved by being smart and definite, and to be vague—they keep telling me—is to be insane, a little unbalanced.

¶ In a plow factory, in the suburbs of the city, there are great tanks in the floor. The tanks are kept filled with many colored liquids. By machinery plows are lifted from the factory floor and swung above the tanks. They are dipped and become instantly and completely black, red, brown, purple, blue, grey, pink.

℄ Can a plow be pink? I have the trick of thinking too rapidly in color. I cannot remember the color of the eyes of my sister. The color of the cheeks of my mistress I cannot remember.

℄ An endless clanking goes on in my head. It is the machinery of the life in which I hang suspended. I and all the men and women in the streets are at this moment being dipped anew in the life of the city. There are no yesterdays for any of us. We hang by a hook in the present. Whatever lies behind this second of conscious time is a lie and I have set myself to lie to the limit. By my lying and by that road only will I succeed in expressing something of the truth of the life into which I also have been flung.

℄ This is evidently true. Plows may not be pink but the prevailing color of the flesh of people is pink. We have all been dipped in a dawn.

℄ Had I not been betrayed by my egotism into trying to fill the blank space in the thought layers in the street my whole life might have been different. But for my act I might have found in the fancy that had come to me the rhythm of my age and got fame like a great man.

¶ I am instead a man of infinite littleness, a maker of words, an eater of food, a weaver of the cast-off clothing of sheep. The gratification to me is that I am so much like you. That is why I understand and love you. I will not however attempt to become your lover. There is destruction in that and we are a long way from being fit to destroy each other. If however we find as we go along that your insanity strikes the same chord as my own something lovely may happen.

A Vagrant

I AM BECOME a brightly colored insect.
I am a boy lying by a river on a summer day.
At my back is an orchard.

¶ I look dreamily out over warm stagnant waters. There is a reed grows out of the yellow mud. In the orchard at my back a hog grunts. An insect with brightly colored back and wings comes swinging down stream. He has lived more freely than the waters of a river. I go with him as I would go in at the door of God's house if I knew the street in which God's house stands, as I would go into you if you would leave the door open for me.

Young Man in a Room

THERE is a woman has just passed the door of my house. There was a barely perceptible quickening of the pulse of my body. "She is beautiful", I thought, and said so aloud. I arose and went to the door to follow her with my eyes. At the moment when I thought her beautiful a wind had just come skipping and shouting down the street. It lifted the woman's hat and she threw up her hand. Her hand made a lovely gesture. My neighbor the wind whispered the story of her beauty to me.

Negro on the Docks at Mobile, Ala.

I HAVE given out of the richness of myself to many mornings.

⁋ At night when the waters of the seas murmured I have murmured.

⁋ I have surrendered to seas and suns and days and swinging ships.

⁋ My blood is thick with surrender, it shall be let out through wounds and shall color the seas and the earth.

⁋ My blood shall color the earth where the seas come for the night kiss and the seas shall be red.

⁋ I have come out and I shall go back.

⁋ I grew and I shall decay.

⁋ I have given myself to days and nights. I have been warm and cold. I have been asleep and awake.

⁋ What you see with your eyes I do not see.

⁋ What you have felt with your fingers creeps unasked through my sleeping body.

¶ I have not gone into your days and your poison has not come into me.

¶ Open my body and drink—my soul is sweet.

¶ I have absorbed suns and seas and days and your poison has not come into me.

Word Factories

LONG AGO an old man sat on a log at the edge of a cornfield and talked to me of God.
His words leaked away.
They would not stay in my head.
The rustling of the leaves of a tree near at hand drowned his voice.
It ran the scale like the voice of an Oriental.
The little drums in my ears were tickled by rising and diminishing waves of sound.

¶ His words ran into the rows of corn and became rows of sounds, an army of sounds.
They hopped and ran like little naked children.

He did not teach me much of God but fragments of God's truth clung to me.

¶ It fell on me like drops of warm rain out of a wet sky.
Did I not learn from him that words are living, breathing things. They are the children of men that have been put to work in a factory. Their little bodies have become bent and stooped and twisted.

¶ The female words have found no lovers. They are barren.
It was not God's wish that it be so.
I am one who would serve God.

¶ Have not my brothers the male words been castrated and made into eunuchs.

¶ I would be nurse to many distorted words.
I would make my book a hospital for crippled words.

¶ From this day I shall wear a white garment and deny myself the pleasures of the body. The words of old time men have been reborn in the factory towns of my country. They are choked with smoke and drowned in waves of new sounds. Will you give a word nourishing food, carry him for a day in the warm body of yourself, as a maid carries with due modesty a babe in her belly.

¶ It is time for the old men to come back out of their sleeping stupor.
They must sit again at the edge of the cornfields.
The words of our lips are being destroyed.
They are undernourished and work in the factories.

¶ There is a tough gnarled new word that has lived for a long time in a corner of my brain. He has set up an insanity there. Sometimes for days I do not dare go near the corner of myself where the word sits crouched, ready to strike, to spring. I start to walk boldly in at the door of my house and then grow afraid and run away.

¶ I run out of the present and into the past.
I run past clanging factory towns, past long bridges, over lakes and seas, into the deserts, into the forests.

¶ It is by chance that I recover and come back into myself.

¶ A twisted word seeks warmth in a corner of my brain. His body is bent and his lips twitch. Something tells me he is the son of an old sweet word born on a hillside long ago in the night.

⁋ They have brought the little twisted word into the West. In the service in which they put him the air was bad. The flying end of a broken wheel hit him and broke his back. His body twitches when he breathes. He lives but the air whines and whistles as it works its way through his lungs. He has escaped from his servitude and has got into my brain.

⁋ My twisted word will live long enough to breed and to perpetuate his kind.

⁋ Bring me quickly the female words that are barren and waiting.

⁋ If you do not hurry, my twisted word will die in the corner of my brain.
I am a breeding place for a twisted word.
I await the time of the breeding.

Man Lying on a Couch

I AM A TREE that grows beside the wall. I have been thrusting up and up. My body is covered with scars. My body is old but still I thrust upwards, creeping towards the top of the wall.

¶ It is my desire to drop blossoms and fruit over the wall.

¶ I would moisten dry lips.

¶ I would drop blossoms on the heads of children over the top of the wall.

¶ I would caress with falling blossoms the bodies of those who live on the farther side of the wall.

The Ripper

I CAN TELL it all quite sanely now.
Look at these hands, how quiet.
Look in these quiet eyes.

¶ I went forth out of this iron house where I have lived.
Myself black with hate,

Mothered I was at the breast of hate.

¶ A knife was in my hand.

¶ I ripped the people open as I came to them,
Slashed them as a pig is slashed on wintry mornings in a farmhouse yard.

¶ Through dreary years I went,
Crawling on my belly in the dark,
Leaping,
Making my knife strokes straight and true.

¶ I cut them open every one.

¶ In each the same dead child.

¶ And then I came to her.
From her a child stepped forth and took my hands,
A quiet child with quiet hands.

¶ Look in these eyes, how quiet.
Look at these quiet hands.

One Who Would Not Grow Old

I HAVE wished that the wind would stop blowing, that birds would stop dead still in their flight without falling into the sea, that waves would stand ready to break upon shores without breaking, that all time, all impulse, all movement, mood, hungers, everything would stop and stand hushed and still for a moment.

¶ It would be wonderful to be sitting on a log in a forest when it happened.

¶ When all was still and hushed, just as I have described, I would get off the log and walk a little.

¶ The insects would all lie still on the ground or float fixed and silent in the air. An old frog that lives under a stone and that had opened his mouth to snap at a fly would sit gaping.

¶ There would be no movement in Chicago, in New York, down by the stock exchange, in towns, in factories, on farms.

¶ Away out in Colorado where a man is at this moment riding his horse furiously striving to catch a steer to be sent to Chicago to be butchered and eaten—

¶ He would stop and the steer would stop.

¶ You and I would walk a little way in the forest or on a prairie and stop. We would be the only moving things in the world and one of us would start a thought rolling and rolling down time, down space, down mind, down life too.

¶ I am sure I would let you do it if later you would be still and keep all the voices of your mind hushed while I did it in my turn.

¶ I would wait ten lives while others did it for my turn.

The New Englander

I TAKE this phone up, then put it down and turn my back.
My fingers grope until they find its lips.

¶ Here now, in this room, the spirit's sword has cut down sharp and clear.

¶ There is as much to be found out as I know or you know. I can put the world down and can turn my back to it. I can cut more worlds out of my silence than you will ever build. I can feel the lips of this thing, can caress its lips. Like David I can tear the lion's jaws apart.

¶ The roaring world in my white hands becomes a pool of whirling soot.

¶ What I want to say to you can be said in fifty ways.

* * *

¶ I have stood at the door of this house now for many years.
I stand here with the knob held in my hand.

¶ I have seen you pass the house, going forward in the street. I have seen snows come and icy winds. In the spring the green things grew for me as I have often said they grew for you. The birds flew past and in the evening darkness settled down.

¶ I have made a stone god of myself, at my back a house, at my hand an open door.

¶ My dream is I shall pass through you into the dawning of new days.

¶ There is my condensed, compressed, distilled desire, to go through doors, to walk in hallways, walled about by life.

The Builder

I AM building me a house slowly—a house in which I may live. Day by day the bricks are piled in long rows making walls. Doors are hung and shingles are being cut for the roof. The air is heavy with the perfume of logs, new cut.

¶ In the morning you may see my house-building—in your street, on the corner there by the church—in the valley beyond your house where the road dips down and crosses a bridge. It is morning and the house is almost complete. Take this key. Go in.

¶ It is evening and my house is in ruins. Weeds and vines have grown on the broken walls. The rafters of the house I aspired to build are buried in long grass. They have decayed. Worms live in them. You will find the ruins of my house in a street of your town, on a country road, in a long street black with smoke clouds in a city.

¶ This is a day, a week, a month, a year. My house is not built. Would you come into my house. Take this key. Come in.

¶ My house is in the perfume of the wild rose that grows by a roadside, it sleeps in the eyes of a nigger who works on the docks at New Orleans. It is built on the foundation of a thought I have not dared to express. I am not subtle enough to build my house. The foundation walls of my house stand on the shivering legs of a little lost dog standing at the closed door of your house on a cold morning in November. The doors of my house creak like the voice of a guinea hen. At night the creaking of the doors of my house is like the voice of a child given over to sadness.

¶ I am building me a house slowly. Take this key. Go in.

Young Man Filled with the Feeling of Power

THE FIRM grip of my fingers on the thin paper of this cigarette is a sign I am very quiet now. Sometimes it is not so. When I am unquiet I am weak but when I am quiet, as I am now, I am very strong.

¶ Just now I went along one of the streets of my city and in at a door and came up here where I am now, lying on a couch and looking out at a window. Very suddenly and completely the knowledge has come to me that I could grip the sides of tall buildings as freely and as easily as I now grip this cigarette. I could hold the building between my fingers, put it to my lips and blow smoke through it. I could blow confusion away. I could blow a thousand people out through the roof of one tall building into the sky, into the unknown. Building after building I could consume as I consume the cigarettes in this box. I could throw the burned ends of cities over my shoulder and out through a window.

¶ It is not often I get in the state I am now in—so quiet and sure of myself. When the feeling comes over me there is a directness and simplicity in me that makes me love myself. To myself at such times I say strong sweet words.

¶ I am on a couch by this window and I could ask a woman to come here to lie with me or a man either for that matter.

¶ I could take a row of houses standing on a street, tip them over, empty the people out of them, squeeze and compress all the people into one person and love that person.

¶ Do you see this hand? Suppose it held a knife that could cut down through all the falseness in you. Suppose it could cut down through the sides of buildings and houses where thousands of people now lie asleep.

¶ It would be something worth thinking about if the fingers of this hand gripped a knife that could cut and rip through all the ugly husks in which millions of lives are enclosed.

A Dying Poet

To Emanuel Carnevali

I FOUND you fighting in the waves of a sea.
A soldier came to my house. His hands were dirty. He had made a mess and besmeared himself. He told me you had thrown yourself into the sea. He said you were fighting desperately to make your way back out of the sea.

¶ I went to the seashore but did not find you.
You were walking in the streets of a city. Something had made you proud and arrogant.

¶ You spoke of a goddess who walks by the seashore in silence. She wears heavy gold wristlets and in her hair is a chain of finely wrought silver.

¶ It was your intention to go on a long journey. We spoke of the matter at length. I watched you closely and understood your most intimate thoughts. You muttered that something had been sacrificed. You spoke of blood that had befouled the grass in the fields.

For a long time I was absorbed in watching you. Your coming cold and in doubt out of the sea did not interest me but your intention of going on a journey was intensely interesting.

Your journey no doubt lasted a lifetime. It lasted through the lifetime of yourself and your father and grandfather.

Wherever you went you bathed yourself. Bathing had become a passion with you.

You bathed in a brook.
You bathed yourself with prayers in a church.
You bathed yourself with love in the presence of men.
You went into a lonely place to bathe yourself with thoughts.

What is the most curious fact of all is that you became an unreality to me. For a long time I had the notion that you had ceased to exist—that you had been blown out like a candle. I thought you had died and that someone had erected a statue to you—that you had become a thing of stone and iron.

I have just found out that you have come out of the sea and home from a journey.

¶ By the shore of the sea there are bushes and I have seen you crawling beneath bushes to look at a goddess who walks by the seashore in silence.

¶ She wears heavy gold wristlets and in her hair is a chain of finely wrought silver.

Brother

GOOD BROTHER, walking up and down, it is my feet you hear running in the shadows by the trees.

¶ You, good brother, are standing by a pig pen at the edge of a field. You are walking in a road behind a threshing engine. You are standing in a dusty place at the mouth of a mine.

¶ Good brother, walking up and down, it is my voice you hear calling to you out of a city.

¶ There is a wild wind.
There is a snow storm whirls about your head.
There is a soft wind that blows down the channel of a river.

¶ There is a dawn has come and you, my brother, are the father of many lovers. You have gone to walk in a dawn.

The Lame One

AT NIGHT when there are no lights my city is a man who arises from a bed to stare into darkness.

¶ In the daytime my city is the son of a dreamer. He has become the companion of thieves and prostitutes. He has denied his father.

¶ My city is a thin old man who lives in a rooming house in a dirty street. He wears false teeth that have become loose and make a sharp clicking noise when he eats. He cannot find himself a woman and indulges in self abuse. He picks cigar ends out of the gutter.

¶ My city lives in the roofs of houses, in the eaves. A woman came to my city and he threw her far down out of the eaves on a pile of stones. Nobody knew. Those who live in my city declare she fell.

¶ There is an angry man whose wife is unfaithful. He is my city. My city is in his hair, in his eyes. When he breathes his breath is the breath of my city.

¶ There are many cities standing in rows. There are cities that sleep, cities that stand in the mud of a swamp.
I have come here to my city.
I have walked with my city.
I have limped slowly forward at night with my city.

¶ My city is very strange. It is tired and nervous. My city has become a woman whose mother is ill. She creeps in the hallway of a house and listens in the darkness at the door of a room.

¶ I cannot tell what my city is like.
My city is a kiss from the feverish lips of many tired people.
My city is a murmur of voices coming out of a pit.

Two Glad Men

First Glad Man

MEN ARE sometimes born who are lords of life and I am one of them.

¶ It is true. What things have I taken from life and will take.

¶ You see me here standing by this fence in a field. The morning sun is shining. There below me, past those trees and down that dusty road, is a town with factory chimneys pouring forth smoke.

¶ There have been hot dry days. The fields are brown and the corn ripens. Sweaty men are between me and the town, toiling in fields, covered with dust.

¶ In the town are houses in long rows. Tired-eyed women are standing by kitchen stoves. They are standing in doorways, looking off over fields, toward me.

¶ It is true and must not be denied. I am one of the lords of life. My belly has received food. It is warm.

¶ I have been drunk with glad-eyed women, receiving me into themselves. I have been drunk with wine, with food, with smells, sights, sounds.

¶ Soft beds have received me.
Soft arms have received me.
Soft nights have sheltered my adventures.

¶ I am neither at the beginning nor at the end. There are no beginnings and no endings.

¶ Hail to thee, sweet life.
Do you hear singing?
Do you smell sweet smells?
Are you erect and ready?

¶ The long day will come unto thee and the night. There shall be the soft pattering of feet on the stairways of houses. There shall be laughter and glad cries.

¶ In my land the time of joy has not come. The gloomy terrible men have denied themselves to the women. They have denied themselves to the stars, to the night winds, to the blustering rains.

¶ The lords of life have been asleep on the hillsides, they have buried themselves away under the corn leaves. They have gone down into mines. They have disguised themselves as workers in factories. They have hidden in houses and shops.

¶ The fat strong men shall come into the land.

There shall be wine drinking.
There shall be love making.
There shall be sweet smells, sweet sounds.

¶ I am but one man but in my loins is the seed that shall be planted in fields and in town. The lords of life shall come into the land.

¶ I await, smiling and laughing.
I lean on this fence.
I look about me.
My eyes are open.
God has opened my eyes.

¶ I am of the breed of the men who shall be the lords over life.
I am glad in the morning.

Answering Voice of a Second Glad Man

¶ Who is singing?
I am singing.

¶ Who is praying?
I am praying.

¶ Who is walking about among people?
I am walking about among people.

¶ Who is hearing voices?
I am hearing voices.

¶ Who is eating ripe fruit?
I am eating ripe fruit.

¶ Who is kissing the maiden in the shadow of the church?
It is I. I am kissing the maiden in the shadow of the church.

¶ For whom are arms opened?
It is for me. Arms are opened to receive me.

¶ Who is in the body of the man I see walking with people, talking with people, embracing the maidens, drinking sweet wines?

¶ I am the man.
I am in the body of the man.
I, the singer, live in his body.

Chicago

TRAINS go out of the city of Chicago and into her sister cities of the valley but the minds of men do not go.

The minds of men do not run out over the flat prairies.
The minds of my brothers stay in their houses.
The fancies of men are bound with iron bands.
They sleep in a prison.

The flesh of women is no longer sweet.
Women are laid in beds.
They have not walked where the wind is.
Their legs have not been caressed by winds that blow low, leaping along, scampering over the ground.

Women weave laces with their fingers and open their breasts to the eyes of the windows but they do not open their eyes to the morning light.

Challenge of the Sea

THE MOUNTAINS shall fall down and the winds go in at the womb of earth ere you shall take me in at the door of your house. Cleanse the doorsteps of houses. Sweeten the air by burning of barks. I am unborn unto you. I sleep unborn in the womb.

¶ You who grope in strange roads may make seas red and spread greens and blues on the walls of your houses but my soul remains untouched by your hands. When your voyage of discovery is ended I shall wriggle out from under your fingers. I shall creep out of your sight. I shall abide in the distance.

¶ What I am at this moment I shall never be again.

¶ Let the madness of that thought creep into your brain.
Suckle your soul at the black breast of defeat.
Accept me as your master.

¶ You have thought me within your grasp. You have thought to take me in at the door of your house.

¶ At night when you have gone to sleep in the arms of a woman I have not slept. When you have cried out in the joy pains of embraces I have stood still, and my stillness has been as the orgasms of gods.

¶ Suppose a stone to arise and sing songs.

¶ Suppose a tree to come out of the ground and go in at the door of a church.

¶ Suppose a man to walk with true reverence where my lips and teeth bite the land.

¶ When the day comes I shall have escaped out of your grasp. When the lids of your eyes lift I shall flee. As the intaking of the breath of a running woman I shall disappear into distances. Only the fluttering fingers of God shall caress my breasts for the stirring of passions. Until the gods arise from their slumbers I shall sleep in the womb.

Poet

To Alfred Steiglitz

HE THREW his weight against the gate. Holding nothing back he hurled himself and there was something lovely to be seen.

¶ With a spring and with all his nerves drawn taut he hurled himself, blood and bone and flesh, against the cold unyielding iron of the gate.

¶ It did begin to yield a little. Inch by inch the gate began to swing. He turned a cut, a bleeding face to look at me and joy shone from his eyes.

¶ The gate swung wide and he walked in and fell into the arms of death.

¶ But there was joy in him.
In a time of little faith joy and love and faith shone from his eyes.

At the Well

IN THE evening I went to the well to drink again. How my bones ached! All the little nerves and muscles of my body cried out.

¶ I had been fighting with God in the long level plain. I ran and ran into a hot dry place and then God came. I fought with him because of the self-satisfaction I saw on his face.

* * *

¶ Had God been substance, had he been a true man I might have laid hold of him. I wrestled all day with a shadow and when afternoon came God smiled again.

¶ Then I went to the well. A few men and women lay on the ground. How softly they talked! There was a negro and a prostitute and two old men who had been robbers.

¶ It was very quiet and peaceful by the well. My hot weary feet touched softly the ground. About the well trees grew and the grass was green. Horses grazed under the trees.

¶ Shall I go again into the plains to fight the self-satisfied God? It is morning and I am thinking now. At the well the negro, the worn-out woman and the two old men are waiting. Knowledge shines out of their eyes. They stay at the well.

An Emotion

To E. P.

SHE WALKED softly in the dust of the road, whispering words. A silver sky dropped down and incircled her head. She was clad in a gold and silver gown.

¶ The little bells were calling, calling.

¶ I ran into the road, plunged into the road. My torn feet were touched by the golden dust of the road. My fingers tore at the gold and silver gown that wrapped her about. With a little whispering laugh she passed into me. I was drawn into her and was healed.

¶ The little bells were calling, calling.

¶ She came with me in at the door of my house. My house stands at the edge of the road, at the edge of the forest. The little tinkling bells sound in the rooms of my house.

¶ The little bells are calling, calling.

Der Tag

I SAW it in the morning when all was silent.
I walked in the streets.

¶ Men and women were silently washing the doorsills of houses. All the openings to the houses were being made clean.

¶ When a guest came in at the door of one of the houses he stooped to kiss the doorsill. Women had brought soft furs and had dropped them on the steps before the houses. Inside the houses the air was warm with life. The floors had been washed. A fragrance arose.

¶ In every eye there was a light shining. Wine was poured forth. Lips met. There was laughter.

¶ Before there had been a great meaningless noise. All was in disorder. The inner walls of houses were black and the doorsills were foul.

¶ Now old walls had broken down and the dust of old walls had settled. The dust had become black fertile soil. Dust to dust and ashes to ashes.

¶ It was a new day. Morning had come.

Another Poet

MY LIFE runs out and out—dancing in the light like the tongue of a serpent.

¶ It goes out and comes back.
My life is a bearer of poison.

¶ I have gone into the plains to poison the well at which I must drink—at which you must drink.

¶ That we must destroy each other is obvious. That does not concern me. The old poets knew that. It was whispered in the shadows of sheep sheds ages ago.

¶ I have thrust out of myself for another purpose.

¶ I am striving to generate a poison that shall be sweeter than the drippings of honey combs, sweeter than the lash of the wind.

A Man and Two Women Standing by a Wall Facing the Sea

First Woman

MY EYES are very small. I cannot see. I look out through narrow slits into a world of light. The world is bathed in light. I cannot see.

¶ My fingers clutch at little warm spots on the broad face of the world. This house is a post stuck in the ground. This tree is a hair growing on the face of a giant.

¶ I cannot see or feel what life is like. My eyes are but two narrow slits into which the light creeps slowly, feeling its way. The light from a lighted world tries to creep into me but the womb of my own life is closed.

¶ I lean against the wall with closed eyes and wait.

¶ Would that the light of life could come clambering in through the narrow closed gate of myself.

¶ Would that the gate could be broken and light come to flood the dark interior of me.

The Man

¶ A god threw up to me out of the sea a little god and I picked it up.

¶ It was thus I became a holy man.
My journeys began.
Holding the little god in my hands I ran.

¶ I ran through houses, through cities, through towns, through halls, through temples. I opened doors and went in. I opened doors and came out. I was a thread held in the hand of a weaver. They wove me. They wove me. They wove me.

¶ I became a holy man.
Their hands beat me. Their hands flayed me.

¶ I knelt in streets, I knelt in silent hills, I knelt by factory doors, on coal heaps, at the mouths of mines, on slag heaps. I crept in at the door of a furnace.

¶ It was then I smelled, tasted and ate.
I have put my teeth in.
Their hands beat me, they flayed me.
Those who knew love and those who were afraid of love flayed me.

¶ The hands came toward me out of the darkness, out of the sunlight. They beat upon me as I knelt in a church. They crept through walls into the room where I had gone to sleep. The hands of children beat me. The doubled fists of men and women beat down upon me.

¶ I became a holy man.
The blood came out of my body. The blood came out of my body as a stream flows in the sunlight.

¶ The hands flayed me like windmills.
The never ceasing hands beat upon me.
My holiness became an insanity.
It became a joy.
It became a relief.

¶ I clung to the little god flung up to me out of the sea.
I became a holy man.

Second Woman

¶ I have crept out of the egg into a wide colorful world.

¶ My hands reach feebly up.
All about me is the color, the smell of life.

¶ There is the color of cut hillsides, of ships sailing, of seas, of riotous death.

¶ I am born—why do I not die and become colorful?
I am born—why am I not born?

¶ Why am I grey?
Why do I build me grey houses and cities?
Why do I wear grey colorless clothes?
Why do I walk always in grey streets?
I am born—why am I not born?
I am feeble—why do I not become strong?
I am young—why do I not become old?
I am very old—why do I not become young?

¶ Why do I not die and fade into colorful splendor.

¶ I have come out of the egg.

¶ I am born.
Why am I not born?

THE END